The
Goan
grind

The Untold Story of Goa's Ground Masalas and Pastes

Perviz De Souza

First published in 2020 by CinnamonTeal Design and Publishing

ISBN 978–93–87676–64–0

BISAC: CKB000000/COOKING/General

CKB044000/COOKING/Regional & Ethnic/Indian & South Asian

Cover design and Typesetting: CinnamonTeal Design and Publishing

Cover and Title Illustration: Malcolm Rebello

CinnamonTeal Design and Publishing
Plot No 16, Housing Board Colony
Gogol, Margao
Goa 403601 India
www.cinnamonteal.in

To Meu Pai and Minha Mãe, for teaching my siblings and
me very early in life to sit at the rogddo to grind, and for
instilling in us the love of an authentic Goan curry.

To my soulmate Zelma, who within weeks of our marriage,
took me shopping - for her own rogddo.

Preface

Goan cuisine is a unique blend of the East and West, influenced by the many cultures that it came into contact with over the centuries. In it, one can identify the distinct influences of Portuguese, African, Arab, Brazilian, Konkani, Malabari and even South-East Asian cultures - a veritable blend of native and foreign culinary styles. The strongest influence - particularly on the Goan Christian cuisine - came from the Portuguese. They introduced into Goa various ingredients that led to a transformation of local recipes and eating habits. Every Goan culinary specialty incorporates four key flavours - heat, acidity, sweetness and salt. Although the Goan Hindu cuisine has its distinct taste, these four key flavours remain the same.

Despite the vast variety of dishes in Goa's culinary collection, it is the staple Goan xitt-coddi (rice and curry) that remains a favourite of all Goans and visitors alike. This tangy and spicy curry has a base that is traditionally ground by hand on a grinding stone. It is usually cooked with a variety of seafood, and sometimes without. It is this base, one amongst the many unique collections of ground masalas or curry pastes, that forms the heart of Goan cuisine.

The traditional Goan rogddo or grinding stone, even today remains the centre around which Goan cooking revolves - both literally and figuratively. No Goan housewife will use anything but a freshly ground masala, finessed with skill and patience into a delicate balance of flavours that only she knows the secret to. This book is a tribute to that humble stone which is the ethos of the Goan culinary life, but is sadly and rapidly disappearing into history.

Prologue

I t was mid-September, a little after the middle of the monsoons. In the ghat section (mountain range) on the Goa-Karnataka border, torrential rains had watered the tree cover, blanketing the mountain slopes with a lush green. The stone cutter and his two sons, guided their donkeys along the treacherous mountain path. They were headed further up the slope, towards the dark and imposing granite rock face. The three men had begun their trek in the early hours of the morning, carrying with them the tools of their trade and a few pieces of plain, dry chapatti tied in a piece of cloth - its bowl shape holding together a little potato bhaji* along with a piece of pickled mango.

Ghanpath came from a family of stone cutters. His task today was to cut a few solid granite blocks to carry back to the little hamlet in which they lived. In a few weeks, devotees (and shoppers), would gather at the famous Colva Fama - Feast of the Infant Jesus - near the city of Margao, about a hundred kilometers away. The fair around the church would offer Ghanpath a good market for his wares - granite grinding stones, mortars and pestles.

The weather gods were being kind to Ghanpath that day. He thanked them for the relatively cool climate as the sun continued to play hide and seek between the clouds. The three men toiled continuously, only taking a short break to have their meagre lunch. By mid-afternoon, they had the roughly hewn granite blocks strapped across the backs of the two donkeys. It was time to head home and rest. They began their precarious journey down the mountain, the animals trudging forward slowly, burdened by the load they carried.

---

*. Bhaji is the Indian term for a vegetable preparation. Chapatti (flat bread) and bhaji is a staple Indian food.

They would begin chiseling away at the strong stone tomorrow, and within a few days the masterpieces that generations of his family were known for would be complete – rogddo or ghonnsunno. A rogddo is a stone grinder, comprising of a mortar and pestle. The mortar is almost semi-circular in shape with a fairly deep varn (bowl) in its centre. The pestle, often called the ghonnsunneacho fator or rogddeacho fator, fits almost perfectly into the bowl. Most of the household grinding is accomplished by a rotatory movement of the pestle in the mortar.

Once the stones were ready, they would be taken to the market. The family's excitement was building as they readied themselves for the long, adventurous and perilous journey across the ghat section to the fair. The bustling market would be a welcome break from the quiet life of their fairly isolated mountain village, and more importantly, it would come with the promise of good earnings and an opportunity to buy much needed household necessities.

                    Perviz De Souza

Chapter 1

The pick of the stone

We were lying in the dust at the far edge of the field. Ghanpath and his sons had picked a spot in the shade of a huge mango tree to set up shop, but sun or shade, we really didn't care. We had braved the elements for years and years, and had been warned by family and neighbours that one day our rugged good looks would catch the eye of the stone cutters. And that is exactly what happened.

I had desperately wanted to get away from the sheer boredom of the mountain and experience the magical moments we had heard of from the kitchens of Goan households. Over the years, stories from these kitchens in villages far away had travelled back to our mountain home. The ancient ones recounted them with pride. And here we were now - my younger cousin and I - in Goa.

Ghanpath had done a great job shaping us for our roles. I was the base - the mortar, and would take the brunt of the work, always bearing the weight of my cousin, Dakto, the pestle. Unfortunately, none of the shoppers paid much attention to us. I must admit that we were still a little rough around the edges, and a little bigger than the others. However, I heard Ghanpath assuring his wife that the lady who finally took us home would put us through a curing process. Patience, I told my cousin. We would certainly find ourselves a home!

We were busy watching Ghanpath and his wife pitch their sales to the stream of shoppers who looked in. I thought they were quite glib with the tongue and did not notice a pretty lady standing off to the side, looking us over. She was decked up in her finest - a shiny red dress and smart shoes. I looked up slyly and realised that she must be newly married for she was still wearing her chuddo - the colorful glass bangles that new brides usually wore. The dashing man standing beside her must be her husband.

Out of the corner of my eye, I saw Ghanpath's petite and charming wife, Savitri, rush towards us. I knew she was going in for the kill. Ghanpath may have disagreed, but as dozens of sales had shown me, she had a far better way with customers than her husband.

"Bai," Savitri addressed the lady respectfully. "Koshhem asa? Tumi novim kazari dista." (Madam, how are you? You must be newly married).

The blush on the lady's cheeks and her shy smile said it all. There was no doubt that Savitri had sealed the deal.

                    Perviz De Souza

Chapter 2

Milagrin's kitchen

The journey to our new home was uneventful, albeit rather bumpy, as the old truck navigated the narrow and winding rural roads. We got home after dark and were dragged into the kitchen. I must admit that we were a little disappointed to find ourselves placed in a corner of Milagrin's fairly large kitchen. It was not the best place to watch the goings-on, but at least we were home. I could see the lady of the house bustling around getting her chores done.

In those days, most families had their cooking spaces on the floor. However, those like Milagrin, who could afford to spend a little more money, built a small kitchen platform from stones. Three single stone walls supported a long slab on which were placed the three-stone chuls or fireplaces. The space below this platform was used as storage for firewood. On one side there was the zodov (firewood), the assortment of lankhdam (big and small pieces of firewood) and pidde (the base of palm leaves). On the other side were usually stored the xirputan (small sticks that were used for kindling) along with sonnam, kotteo and kholio (coconut husks, shells and dried leaves).

Those were the days of clay cooking pots and in some kitchens, a few copper utensils. Although these clay pots may appear to be cheap and rudimentary today, the food cooked in them has a flavour of its own. Families would usually purchase their clay utensils at local fairs or the more prominent weekly markets. You could gauge the age and use of a clay vessel by its blackened sides - the old and seasoned vessels being the prized possessions of housewives.

The next morning, Milagrin began sorting out her purchases from the fair. She had picked provisions that included bunches of onions and chilies along with a few clay utensils. She threw open her kitchen window and soon we could hear her animated conversation with the neighbours. Filled with excitement, she was recounting her experiences at the Fama and telling them of her new acquisition.

"Wouldn't they like to see her new rogddo?" She asked.

And before we knew it, the kitchen was a hive of activity - chatter, poking, prodding, and some rolling - as the women checked the feel of the stone. Milagrin offered them some traditional khajem (sweets) and roasted grams from the fair. It appeared that she was being very hospitable and generous, obviously with some motive in mind. And then she threw the question.

"How do you prepare the stones for grinding?" She asked coyly.

Again, after much conversation and discussion, one of the older ladies - obviously the matriarch of the village - finally pronounced with authority.

"Get some paddy husks and soak some rice. We'll come by tomorrow morning and get it done."

So tomorrow we would be put through the grind. I knew it was going to be a restless night for me.

     Perviz De Souza

Chapter 3

Preparing the stone

We were up at the cock's crow; in fact, we had barely slept. Dakto and I had been up most of the night discussing what the day would have in store for us. Milagrin too was up earlier than usual. The Angelus bell of the village church broke through the quiet of the early morning. Milagrin crossed herself and automatically stopped all she was doing to recite the ancient Marian prayer. The bell rang three times in sets of 3, each set followed by a pause. The ninth stroke was a signal for people to get out and go to work. Milagrin was ready to begin.

She started a fire and set a pot of water for boiling. The next step was getting some breakfast ready for the neighbours, who would be arriving soon. Milagrin carried a bankim (a low stool) and placed it next to us along with a malti (shallow clay bowl) with the soaked rice, a small pantulo (basket) with paddy husks, a little kollsuli (small copper pot) filled with water and a pelo (brass cup). She wanted to ensure that everything was ready before the women arrived.

Soon the matriarch made her appearance and Milagrin greeted her with great joy.

"Dev boro dis diun, Rojinmai." She said, greeting the matriarch respectfully and quickly poured her a cup of tea. It was apparent that Rojinmai was a veteran in the tasks of the kitchen. Without much ado, she sat in front of us to see that everything was the way she wanted it to be. Soon a few more ladies walked in and Rojinmai set into action.

The lady sitting on the stool washed us first, using a polished kotti (coconut shell) to scoop out the water. She poured a few handfuls of paddy husk into my varn, added water and skillfully began rolling Dakto around. Oh, that hurt! Being ground against each other was something we had never experienced before. It would definitely take some getting used to. After all, we were made for that and for each other.

The women took turns - chattering, laughing, humming and grinding the husks until Rojinmai instructed them to begin grinding the rice instead. So, it continued through the better part of the morning, until the rice paste was clean white and the women were sure that there was no more stone sediment left over to spoil the curry pastes that Milagrin would soon be grinding.

Finally they were done. Cheerfully calling their goodbyes, the women left the kitchen. Sore all over, but washed clean, we looked forward to an evening of quiet and peace. I am sure that Milagrin felt the same.

                              Perviz De Souza

<h1 align="center">Chapter 4</h1>

<h1 align="center">Curry in a hurry</h1>

Milagrin's family was well known for their culinary skills. The gossip around was that there weren't many women who could match the rich flavours of the Goan masalas that her mother produced. Milagrin had learnt the tricks from a master and she was eager to begin.

We watched as she sat astride an adollo (a low, wooden stool on which a c-shaped, metal blade is fixed), and deftly scaled and gutted some mackerel, cutting them into fairly large pieces, seasoned with salt and set them aside.

Then, taking a maltulo (a small earthen clay bowl), she began to throw in the ingredients for her fish curry paste, reciting by rote the condiments.

- 5-6 Kashmiri chilies
- A small piece of ginger
- 3 garlic cloves
- 5-6 peppercorns
- 1 teaspoon coriander seeds
- Small ball of tamarind soaked in water
- 1/2 teaspoon turmeric powder
- 1/2 teaspoon cumin
- 1 green chilly
- Salt
- A few sliced bimbli*

Sitting at the adollo again, she used the kantollem (a grater at the tip of the adollo's blade) to grate the flesh of a whole coconut into the maltulo.

"Chun kantum zallem," she sang to herself. Continuing her humming, she approached us, poured the contents of the bowl all over me and began to grind. Her movements were swift and there was a certain rhythm in her work. I must say, we were happy to be of use again. She was our master now and we, her servants. In a matter of minutes, she had ground the condiments into a thin paste, and a spicy odour filled the air.

Milagrin went to the traditional chul and placed a kunnllem (a clay cooking pot) on the fire. Using a funkpachi nolli (small piece of metal pipe), she blew into the fire until it was blazing well. Walking out to the backyard, she then plucked a few bimbli that would give an acidic hit to the dish. She was ready to cook her fish curry.

(*Commonly known as cucumber tree or tree sorrel, bimbli is a natural souring agent and popular in Goan cuisine.)

Perviz De Souza

Chapter 5

Green with envy

Days went by but our routine stayed the same. Milagrin dutifully ground her coconut curry almost every day. Other than that, we had nothing to do and felt rather lonesome in our corner.

Then, one morning, things changed. Instead of picking the dry, red chilies, we were surprised to see Milagrin tossing some fresh, green ones into her malti. We knew today would be different - the lady of the house was preparing a green masala. As always, with practiced ease, she prepared her ingredients.

- 12-15 medium sized green chilies
- 2 cups of diced fresh coriander
- 2 teaspoons coriander seeds
- 2 inch piece of ginger
- 12 garlic cloves
- 1 teaspoon cumin
- 1 teaspoon peppercorns
- 8 cloves
- 2 inch piece of cinnamon
- 1 teaspoon turmeric
- 1 medium onion (chopped fine)
- 1 cup palm vinegar
- Sprinkling of sugar

The difference this time around was that Milagrin used no water. Instead, she judiciously poured coconut vinegar as she continued to grind the condiments into a rich, green paste. The acidity of the vinegar and the spicy aroma of the chilies, brought tears to her eyes and ours too. Once done, she used the remaining vinegar to wash away the ground paste. Not wanting any trace of the curry to remain on our rough surface, she washed us thoroughly with water, scooping it away until we were almost dry.

Milagrin filled the green masala paste into a bhorni (a ceramic jar), where the coconut vinegar would help preserve it for a while.

Today's lunch promised to be different - we wondered what the celebration was for.

　　　　　　　　Perviz De Souza

Chapter 6

Synonymous with Goa - Recheado masala

Milagrin's mother always reminded her children that no Goan kitchen was complete without a good stock of Recheado masala - the spicy-sweet-tangy Goan curry paste with a deep, red colour. It is a mix of spices with red chilly as the main ingredient. In Portuguese, the word recheado means 'to stuff' and though the masala is traditionally used to stuff fish, especially mackerel and pomfret, it is also used in many other Goan dishes. Since her mother was visiting, it seemed like there was no better time than now to get it done.

"Mai", Milagrin called sweetly. "Since you are here today, can we make some recheado masala, please? My masala never really turns out as good as yours!"

"Do you have some good palm vinegar?" asked her mother. No Goan housewife worth her salt would grind a recheado without this staple ingredient.

"Yes, Mai. I have some that you gave me during my last visit home." She replied and reached down into her cupboard for the garrafão (a glass jar of 5 litres used to store feni or vinegar), filled with a deep, yellow liquid. Milagrin's mother pulled off the stopper that was made with a piece of bamboo wrapped in an old cloth. Pouring a little into the palm of her hand, she tasted it, nodding her approval.

"Let's get started," she said. With her daughter's help, she began putting the ingredients together into a malti.

- 20 Kashmiri chilies, broken into small pieces
- 3/4 teaspoon turmeric powder
- 1 teaspoon cumin seeds
- 15 peppercorns

- 6 cloves
- 1 inch piece of cinnamon
- 10 garlic cloves, peeled
- 1 inch piece of ginger
- A small ball of tamarind

Into this, she poured half a cup of palm vinegar and kept it aside for about 30 minutes. While the vinegar seeped into this mix, the two of them shared a cup of tea and caught up on family gossip.

After sometime, Milagrin's mother herself sat to grind the paste. Her movements were swift and vigorous as she continued talking to Milagrin, who was squatting on the floor just next to us. Our eyes smarted with the smell of chilly. Of course, we were not alone; Milagrin too was dabbing her eyes with the corner of her sleeve. Her mother tasted the paste, and threw in about a teaspoon of sugar and a little salt, and continued grinding until the seasoning mixed in well.

And then it was done. What a relief!

　　　　　　　　Perviz De Souza

Chapter 7

Grinding for sannas

It was the eve of the feast at the village church and Milagrin had just returned home after the mass and novenas. Tomorrow was a big day for the villagers. Earlier that day, Salu, the village toddy-tapper, had passed by and left two bottles of fresh sur (coconut toddy), by the kitchen door. Some of the coconut palms behind the house were being tapped and we could smell the toddy every morning. Milagrin picked up the bottles and sniffed them. Pouring a little of the milky white liquid into a pelo, she tested its freshness. She smacked her lips, poured a little more and slowly sipped the sur. It was just right!

Toddy is an essential ingredient in making sannas - a steamed rice and coconut bread that usually has a slightly sweet taste from the fresh coconut toddy* that is added as a fermenting agent into the batter. Traditional Goan delicacies like sorpotel and xacuti are best eaten with sannas. She would have to work late today to grind for the sannas and get the batter ready.

Milagrin had soaked 2 cups of ghanvti ukdde tandool (parboiled rice) earlier that day. She first drained all the water from the rice. Carrying this to the adollo, she cracked open a coconut, pouring its milk into the rice. She then scraped half the coconut into a second malti.

Once done, she ground the rice into a fine paste and then grinding the coconut to a similar consistency, mixed the two pastes together. She then mixed in the toddy along with some sugar and began to mix the batter. I must say, the smell of toddy was rather strong - almost intoxicating. However, it certainly was a welcome change from the pungent, masala odours.

Milagrin poured out the batter into a moddki (an earthen pot used for cooking rice), and using the rest of the toddy, slowly began thinning it into a light batter. Not satisfied with the taste, she added a sprinkling of salt and a little more sugar. Covering the bowl with a clean, damp cloth, she left it aside to ferment and rise.

Steaming the sannas was a time-consuming task, but they tasted best when they were fresh. Tomorrow there would be enough time to make the sannas, but she would need to rise earlier than usual to complete steaming them.

(*Yeast can be used as a fermenting agent where toddy is not available.)

                    Perviz De Souza

Chapter 8

The village feast

We were still asleep when the loud explosions reverberated through the air. It was the fesatcho-dis (feast day) and the foznem (dynamite petards) were sure to awaken every villager - young and old. It was that time of the year when the entire village would be out in its finery, heading for the feast mass and then wandering around for a while in the feira (fair). Milagrin rushed into the kitchen full of excitement in anticipation of the day ahead. There was a lot of cooking to be done as the house was packed with guests. Milagrin had planned her feast menu beforehand. The sorpotel had matured well over the last few days, but she still had to get her add-maas and arroz done. And the sannas too. She had been up late last night, making the preparations and her last task before going to bed had been grinding the rice for the sannas. Now, the steaming wouldn't really take long.

As she lit up the fire, the plaintive sounds of brass instruments could be heard in the distance. It was the alvorada (the brass band), heralding the start of festivities at the break of dawn. The little ones too were up early that day. We could hear their shouts of joy as they ran to the balcão (balcony), waiting for the brass band to make its way through the village. As they neared, it became obvious that the performers were not at their best, some of the instruments did not seem to be in sync with the others. But no one really cared - everyone was in a celebratory mood.

Milagrin shouted out to someone, reminding them that the dresses for the feast needed to be ironed. Also, could her husband please take her jewellery out of the cupboard? After all, she had to look her best!

The entire family had gathered for the feast celebration. Milagrin was excited about taking her little nephew to the festachem mis (feast mass) and later, to the fair. She had diligently attended the salves (the nine day novena), and was particularly impressed by the fiery pregador (preacher) invited to the village. The feast mass would definitely take longer but there was no way she would miss it.

We knew that the fair would not be as grand as the one we had experienced at the Colva Fama. The likes of Ghanpath always found such fairs relatively small to set up shop. But the food stalls would be there and the games stalls too. This was enough excitement for the villagers. We were sure that Milagrin would return with some traditional feast fare - kaddeo-boddeo (the sticky jaggery and sugar coated sticks) along with some chonne (chickpeas roasted in a clay oven).

But there were more important tasks to complete before that. She had to steam the sannas.

It was now 8.00 am and the high mass for the feast was scheduled for 10.30 am. Milagrin looked worried. Would she have enough time to get all her cooking done?

She pulled out a komfro (a large copper steamer) and after washing it clean, set it on the fire. Filling small moulds with batter - ensuring enough space was left for the batter to rise - she let them steam for about 15 minutes. As the first batch of the fluffy sannas was out of their moulds, Milagrin bit into one and her face filled with joy. She was very pleased with herself. After all, this was the first time she had made these traditional rice cakes on her own.

"These sannas will be a wonderful accompaniment to the sorpotel Mai made." Milagrin said to her husband who walked in just then. "Maybe I should try to make a few goddache sandon too, since I still have some batter left."

"I don't think you have time for that," her husband replied. "It's getting late. We have to get ready and leave for the church soon." However, Milagrin was not one to give up that easily. She quickly grated some coconut and a piece of palm jaggery into a malti. She then added a pinch of cardamom powder and mixed the filling

        Perviz De Souza

well. For the last batch, she poured a little less batter into the moulds and sprinkled a generous helping of the coconut-jaggery filling on the top, covering it with some more batter. She left them to steam while she rushed to get ready.

We could hear the pealing of the church bells, announcing that the mass was about to begin. Milagrin rushed, took the komfro off the heat and checked that there was nothing left on the fire. She looked stunning in a bright blue, floral dress. Milagrin was pretty and would certainly turn some heads today.

Chapter 9

Dodol - a sweet treat

Soon we were approaching Christmas and the kitchen was buzzing with activity. Milagrin had called in some of the neighbours to help out with the preparations. For a change, the grinding now was for traditional Christmas sweets. One of the ladies gave us a good scrub using some kato (coconut coir), ensuring all the remnants of the masala were removed. Then, the grinding began and went on throughout the day. I lost count of the number of rounds of plain coconut or local rice that went through me. We ached all over from the constant grinding.

Coconut juice is the main ingredient in many of these sweets. However, the one being prepared today was dodol - a jelly like sweet that is a must for Christmas. The ladies worked well as a team, accustomed to doing these tasks together. Once again it was Rojinmai who took charge, calling out the ingredients so that the other ladies could get them ready.

- 1 ½ cups parboiled rice flour*
- 16 cups of milk from 4-5 coconuts (thick and thin juice)
- 1/2 teaspoon cardamom powder
- 6 pyramids of palm jaggery
- 1 cup cashew nuts (chopped)
- Ghee
- Salt for seasoning

The women got to the task. While one greased the pans that would be used for the sweet, the other started with the grinding. The first round of coarse grinding yielded around 8 cups of thick milk. Now, 8 cups of hot water was added to the coconut and it was

---

*. Nachne (ragi) flour is also used in some versions

        Perviz De Souza

ground again, this time extracting 8 cups of thin milk. The milk was kept in separate bowls.

Rojinmai's voice boomed through the kitchen. "Melt and strain the jaggery. And one of you, mix the flour with the thin coconut milk." The aroma of melting jaggery filled the air.

"Get the jaggery pan on the fire and let's start adding in the flour paste, little by little. Keep stirring. We don't want the mixture sticking to the side of the pan."

Rojinmai tasted the mixture and sprinkled a little salt for seasoning. The women took turns stirring this mix, slowly adding in the thick coconut milk until the mixture thickened and began leaving the sides of the pan.

Once again, Rojinmai tested the mixture and nodded her approval. "Mix in the cardamom powder, cashew nuts and ghee. Keep stirring, it's almost done. There are no more bubbles left, which means there is no more moisture."

In a few minutes, the rich, silky mixture was taken off the fire and poured into the greased pans. One of the ladies used a greased spoon to smoothen up the top. The dodol was ready and left to cool.

Chapter 10

Pinagra – the sweet for tea time

The women worked with vigour for there was much to be done. The traditional khuswar or spread of Christmas goodies, contained as many as 22 sweets. The pinagra or pinaca was next. This sweet is made with local, red parboiled rice, coconut, jaggery and cardamom powder. Under Rojinmai's directions, the women set to work.

First, they got all the ingredients together. Surprisingly, I must say, there weren't many.

- 2 cups of local parboiled rice
- 2 pyramids of palm jaggery (about 250 grams)
- 2 cups of freshly grated coconut
- 1/2 cup water
- 1/2 teaspoon cardamom powder

One of the ladies cleaned and washed the rice thoroughly, spreading it out on an old cloth to dry in the sun. Once the rice was considered to be dry enough, the ladies roasted it on a kail (a frying pan) and set it aside to cool. Another lady brought out the dantem (a traditional millstone), and placed it on the centre of the floor. She began grinding the rice until she had a nice, grainy powder.

Rojinmai called out, "Keep a few spoonfuls of rice flour aside for later."

While the grinding was happening, the others had scraped the jaggery into a malti, added the fresh, grated coconut into it and pounded the cardamom seeds in an amaldosto (a brass pounder). Adding all three ingredients into a kail with a little water, Rojinmai placed the pan on the fire until the jaggery melted.

After this, one of the ladies washed us thoroughly, soaking off all the water with a piece of cloth. She then began to grind the jaggery-coconut mixture into a fine paste. Rojinmai tested its consistency with her fingers. Seemingly satisfied, she asked the ladies to slowly mix in the flour until it turned into a nice dark brown, sticky dough.

"Let's take a break." She called. "We must let the mixture cool and dry for some time."

After a while, the ladies were back on the job. Moistening their palms, they began to roll the dough into small, cylinder shapes, dusting them with the rice flour that had been set aside.

The pinagra was ready!

Chapter 11

Doce de Grão – the sweet treats continue

The making of the khuswar continued through the day. The women seemed determined to get the sweets done before nightfall. As we understood later, they had an arrangement to get together and make sweets in yet another house before Christmas. Now, Milagrin was discussing the requirements for making the popular doce de grão, locally known as chonya doce. Rojinmai immediately replied, "The ingredients aren't many, but making it requires a lot of patience and your hands are going to hurt from all the stirring. We also need time to soak the dal." Inspite of this piece of news, the women were not deterred, least of all, Milagrin. How could she have a Christmas khuswar without the doce?

The ingredients as Rojinmai had mentioned were few.

- 250 grams of chana dal (split Bengal gram)
- 200 grams of fresh, grated coconut
- 450 grams of sugar
- 1/2 teaspoon cardamom powder
- 1 ½ tablespoons of ghee
- Salt for seasoning

One of the ladies quickly washed and soaked the chana dal. Since it would need to stay that way for three to four hours, the group moved on to the preparation of some other sweets, including kulkuls and kormolan. By the time they were done, the dal was ready.

After cooking the chana dal until it was tender, one of the ladies ground it into a thick and smooth paste. She then ground the grated coconut into an almost dry paste. Pouring the dal into a kail, Rojinmai instructed the women to add in the coconut paste, sugar and salt. Now this mixture had to be cooked on a medium heat with continuous stirring. It popped and fumed like a volcano crater ready to erupt, but kept thickening. Eventually, after much stirring, the mixture began to leave the sides of the kail and come together like a ball. One of the ladies, deftly dropped in the ghee and the cinnamon powder, and continued stirring until it all blended into one. The piping hot mixture was now poured out onto a greased tabletop and with the aid of a lattnni (rolling pin), spread out evenly in a thick layer.

Milagrin then cut the dough into neat, diamond shapes and left them to cool.

Her khuswar was done and soon it would be time to celebrate!

Chapter 12

Christmas time, Sorpotel time!

It was a few days before Christmas, and despite the morning chill, there was a buzz in the air. Milagrin wanted to ensure that she had the best table at Christmas. She had learnt from her mother that one should begin the preparations early on, especially with pork specialties. Her mother always said, "Maas pikonkzai," which meant the dish had to mature.

Over the last few days, we had watched the women gather together and get most of the traditional Christmas sweets, called the consuada or khuswar, done. But we had taken almost no part in the preparations. With those out of the way, Milagrin was now ready to get started with the savouries.

That morning the village maaskar (butcher), had delivered fresh pork to the kitchen door. Milagrin's husband was chattering with excitement at the breakfast table as they discussed the sorpotel that was to be made today.

Watching Milagrin at work, it was clear that the making of this specialty was a labour of great love. The recipe had to be followed meticulously and the work was hard.

Milagrin pulled out her book of recipes to check the ingredients. First, the masala.

- 2 inches of cinnamon
- 1 tablespoon black peppercorns
- 2 teaspoons cloves
- 2 teaspoons cumin seeds
- 2 inches of fresh ginger
- 10 garlic cloves
- 5 Byadagi chilies

     Perviz De Souza

- 15 dry Kashmiri chilies (for their red color)
- 2 small marble-size balls of tamarind (soaked in sufficient water)
- Palm vinegar (as required during grinding)

Then, the meat.

- 1/2 kg pork
- 1/2 kg liver and kidney
- 1/4 cup pork blood

And finally, the rest of the ingredients.

- 4 large onions (chopped)
- 8-10 garlic cloves (chopped)
- 1 inch of fresh ginger (chopped)
- 2 green chilies (sliced)
- 3-4 tablespoons of sugar or Goan palm jaggery
- Palm vinegar (to balance the acidity)
- Salt (to season)

Milagrin washed the meat well, seasoning it with salt and vinegar. She then added it to a pot with some water and set it to boil. Since that would take time, she decided to leave it on the fire and get on with the other tasks at hand. With the masala ingredients in her malti, Milagrin quickly ground them with vinegar and set that aside. The spices, chilly and vinegar had by now become a part of our lives and we enjoyed their sharp, tangy odours. Taking the meat off the fire, she let it cool for a while and then cut it into very small cubes, making sure she kept each of the meats, including the fat, in different bowls. She then shallow fried them separately.

Milagrin set a touli (a shallow clay utensil) on the fire. Adding oil to it, she fried the onions until they were translucent. She then added the green chilies, ginger and garlic, continuing to fry the ingredients for a few more minutes. To this she added the masala and let it cook for about five minutes. Next added in were the fried meats, the blood and the stock from boiling the meat. She let this cook on low heat until the gravy reached a fairly thick consistency. After about 45 minutes, Milagrin tasted the preparation and seasoned it with salt, sugar and vinegar until she was satisfied. Finally, with a cheeky look around to ensure that no one saw her, she added a few spoonfuls of coconut feni and let it cook for another 10 minutes.

The sorpotel was now ready and its aroma filled the air. Milagrin wiped the sweat off her brow and smiled. She knew her husband would walk in soon - he never could resist eating sorpotel, and this was as good as her mother's!

                    Perviz De Souza

Chapter 13

Vindalho de Porco

Milagrin had saved a good portion of the pork (about a kilogram) to make a vindalho, another Goan favourite, but far easier to prepare than the sorpotel. While many would take the easy way out by using the recheado masala already prepared, Milagrin preferred to go with her grandmother's recipe and have everything made fresh again.

Her masala ingredients included,

- 12 Kashmiri chilies
- 1 teaspoon cumin seeds
- 1/2 teaspoon black peppercorns
- 1 cinnamon stick
- 6 cloves
- 1/2 teaspoon turmeric powder
- 12 garlic cloves, chopped
- 2 teaspoons ginger, chopped
- Palm vinegar (as required to balance the acidity)

Milagrin returned to her bankim and ground the masala ingredients into a fine paste, using enough vinegar to ensure it didn't turn too dry. Using additional vinegar to wash off the remaining paste, she put it aside for later use in her cooking.

Next, she cut the meat into fairly large cubes (about a square inch), then washed and salted it. Marinating the meat with a generous amount of vindalho masala, she left it aside. The longer it marinated, the better it would taste.

The cooking part was fairly easy. Dice four onions and a couple of green chilies. Saute these in a little oil, then add the marinated meat and let it cook some more. Her grandmother had taught her never to add any water but to cover the tizal with a mandd (a round, flat wooden lid), and let the meat cook in its own steam, on low heat. The fat would melt, keeping the meat moist and tender. If required, she could season it again with a little salt and sugar. And for a little more of an acidic hit, she could always add a dash of the masala vinegar she had set aside.

Perviz De Souza

Chapter 14

Galinha Cafreal for Christmas

By Christmas Eve, most of the sweets were ready and it was time to prepare for a sumptuous Christmas lunch. Milagrin had been talking to the other women about a cafreal - something we had not heard of before.

The mention of cafreal resulted in a little discussion. One of the ladies said that she had heard from her grandmother that cafreal originated in Mozambique (another Portuguese colony), and was the marinade for a popular dish called Frango Piri-Piri. The Portuguese developed a taste for this dish and carried the recipe back to Goa. Here, it underwent some changes, especially the addition of more spice. But it didn't matter to Milagrin; it sounded just right for her Christmas menu.

Milagrin brought out her recipe book wanting to make sure she had all the ingredients right. She picked up her favourite bowl and began to toss in the ingredients for the cafreal marinade.

- A bunch of fresh coriander leaves, chopped coarsely
- 1 tbsp whole black peppercorns
- 8-10 cloves
- 10 green chilies
- 1 stick of cinnamon, about 2 inches
- 1 teaspoon of cumin seeds
- 1/2 teaspoon turmeric powder
- A piece of fresh ginger
- 6-8 cloves garlic
- Palm vinegar to balance the acidity

Milagrin ground the masala ingredients into a fine wet paste and set that aside.

Earlier Milagrin had chopped her chicken into large chunks. Scoring the meat, she left it to rest after seasoning with salt, some lemon juice, and a little ginger-garlic paste. Now, she covered these chunks in the rich, green paste and set them aside to marinate.

That evening she heated a large saucepan and when the oil was hot enough, she arranged the chicken pieces over the oil. Next, she covered the pan and let the meat cook for about 8 minutes on low fire. Opening the pan, she checked the seasoning and flipped the pieces over, placing the cover back on to let them cook evenly on the other side.

Then, uncovering the pan, she let the gravy thicken over a low fire. As the pieces of chicken began to brown, the kitchen was filled with a rich aroma.

Tomorrow, the Galinha Cafreal was sure to be the show-stopper at the Christmas table.

Perviz De Souza

Chapter 15

Going vegetarian - Chonya Ros

One evening, a Hindu neighbour, Swati, came over to visit. Soon the discussion turned to the differences between Hindu and Christian culinary preparations. Swati too was an accomplished cook, and Milagrin absolutely loved some of her cooking.

"Will you teach me to prepare a chonya ros?" She asked Swati.

Swati was most happy to oblige. "You'll have to soak the chonne (chickpeas) tonight," she informed Milagrin. "You do that and I'll come help you cook it tomorrow morning."

So Milagrin poured a cupful of chickpeas into a malti (large earthen bowl) and adding about 3 cups of water, left it to soak overnight. She was always eager to learn something new.

By mid-morning the next day, Swati was at the door. The first thing she did was to drain the water, rinse the chickpeas again and set them to boil with a little salt for seasoning. "They have to be nice and soft," she advised Milagrin.

"Now, let's get started on the masala," she continued.

With Swati calling out instructions, Milagrin began to collect the ingredients into a malti.

- 1 onion, diced
- 1/4 cup coriander leaves
- 1 tablespoon garam masala
- 1/4 teaspoon fennel seeds
- 1/2 cup freshly grated coconut

Swati set a kunnllem on the fire and adding a little oil, sauteed the onions until they turned translucent and caramelized. Letting them cool a while, she then roasted the coriander, garam masala, fennel seeds and coconut, and poured the roasted ingredients and ½ tsp turmeric powder into my varn. Her touch felt different; in fact, her movements as she rolled Dakto around seemed sharper and well-rehearsed. But she had the paste ground real quick.

"We'll also need a few other ingredients." She called to Milagrin.

- 3 tablespoons of oil
- 1 teaspoon mustard seeds
- 8-10 curry leaves
- 1 tomato, chopped
- 2-3 green chilies

Setting the kunnllem on the fire again, she heated some oil and threw in the mustard seeds. Once they began to splutter, in went the curry leaves and green chilies. To this, she then added the masala paste and sauteed it for about 5 minutes until the oil separated. The chopped tomato went in next and was cooked until it turned mushy.

Swati then added the boiled chickpeas and stirring continually, cooked them for about 10 minutes until the gravy thickened, adding a little more salt, and the juice of a small ball of tamarind to achieve the desired taste.

She let Milagrin have a spoonful from the koddiecho doulo (a shallow ladle made of a coconut shell and a bamboo stick).

Milagrin's face lit up as she savoured the many flavours. "Dev borem korum, Swati," she said. "It is delicious!"

 Perviz De Souza

Chapter 16

Milagrin makes a Xacuti

Chicken was a luxury in Milagrin's household. Only a celebration of some sort called for the killing of a prized fowl. So, when the slaughtered and defeathered bird was brought into the kitchen, I looked at Dakto and said, "Seems like there is a special occasion."

We saw Milagrin pick up her recipe book and begin flipping through the pages. However, the disappointed look on her face told us that something was wrong. She slammed the book shut and threw it on the table exclaiming angrily to herself, "I can't find the recipe for xacuti."

She paced around the kitchen, trying to figure out a solution. And then, she remembered! One of the neighbours, Bella, was known for her xacuti. She decided to seek her help.

Milagrin was a charming person and was soon back with Bella in tow.

"Let's get the xacuti masala ready first as we have to grind it into a powder on the dantem," said Bella. With the visiting chef calling out the instructions, Milagrin set about putting the ingredients together.

Ingredients:

- 1 kg coriander seeds
- 1/4 kg khuskhus (poppy seeds)
- 1/4 kg crushed turmeric pieces
- 750 gms fennel
- 100 gms fenugreek
- 100 gms mustard seeds

- 100 gms peppercorns
- 50 gms cumin seeds
- 100 gms cloves
- 150 gms cinnamon sticks
- 20 gms mace
- 10 gms star anise
- 20 gms cardamom
- 10 nutmegs
- 10 gms bay leaves
- 10 gms caraway seeds
- 750 gms small red chilies, ghanvti (local)

Setting a koili (frying pan) on the fire, she roasted all the spices together, leaving the crushed turmeric and coriander seeds to be roasted separately. Then, sitting at the dantem, they took turns grinding the spice mixture into a fine powder. Milagrin filled the xacuti masala powder into a large glass jar for later use and set about grinding for the curry.

It was not often that we saw a dantem in use. It was a set of two grinding stones placed on each other. As I watched, I realised that this kind of dry grinding would not be possible with Dakto and I.

Sitting at the adollo, Bella grated a coconut and asked Milagrin to begin roasting it on the tovo (a flat pan normally used for frying chapatti or kailoieo - a type of pancake made of rice batter), and using a kailontto (a metal ladle), stirred until it turned a nice brown colour. She quickly grated another half coconut and then pouring it into my varn, began grinding. Bella finished by straining out the thin juice from the coconut and setting it aside.

"Milagrin," she called, "add three kulers (spoons) of the xacuti masala into the roasted coconut and start grinding."

While the grinding continued, Bella added some salt and turmeric powder to the cut chicken pieces along with the paste of ginger, garlic, coriander and green chilies.

     Perviz De Souza

As Milagrin began grinding, we sensed the difference. I could smell the rich aroma of the roasted spices; their oils released and blending into one another. As the condiments were squeezed between Dakto and me, we could feel the heat of the ghanvti chilies burning into us. As soon as the grinding was done, Milagrin handed the curry paste over to Bella, who had already begun sauteing some chopped onions. She dropped the marinated chicken into the pot, added the xacuti masala with some water and let it cook.

A rich, spicy aroma filled the air and we could see Milagrin smiling. She certainly was pleased!

Chapter 17

Getting ready for the rains

We knew that like every other Goan, Milagrin and her husband could not do without their fish for every meal. It was early summer and by the first week of June, the monsoons would descend on Goa in all their fury. We watched as Milagrin fussed around the kitchen getting everything ready. She knew the rains meant that due to the rough waters, the fishermen would not venture out into the sea until mid-August. The only fish available would be the ones caught off the shore by the locals using either a shintari (the traditional bamboo fishing rod) or kantaie (nets dropped a little away from the shore). However, this fish would always be short in supply and hence, very expensive.

Like all Goan housewives, Milagrin had already prepared her purmento - stocking up for the monsoons with spices, onions, salt, dried fish, etc. She now wanted to take it a step further and use a well-known curing technique to preserve some of the fish for use during the long, rainy season. She would make some para but first she had to decide which fish she would use. Since both she and her husband loved mackerel, she decided to go with it.

We watched as Milagrin looked through her stocks of kharem (dried fish) and finally took out about 25 pieces of dried mackerel from the tin in which they were stored. She needed to make sure that the fish was exceptionally well dried, so she tied them by their tails on a sutli (twine) and strung them between two trees in the backyard. To ensure that the crows would not eat any, she strung up a few pieces of metal too - the rattling would scare the birds away. The sun would make the fish nice and crisp in just a couple of days.

Every morning she would put the fish out to dry and dutifully bring them in before nightfall. After three days, she felt the fish and knew they were just right. For good measure, she now cut off their heads and tails and gutted them. Spreading them on a bamboo mat on the ground, she left them to dry for another day. Now to get the pickling done.

She got her ingredients ready in a bowl.

- 35-40 Kashmiri chilies
- 4 inch cinnamon stick
- 20 big garlic cloves
- 4 inch piece of ginger
- A spoonful of peppercorns
- 40 cloves
- 4 inches cinnamon
- 1 teaspoon mustard seeds
- 2-3 tablespoons cooking oil

She also measured out about 1½ litres of coconut vinegar from the garrafão.

Milagrin got working on her masala. Twisting the stems off some 40 red chilies, she washed them in two cups of vinegar (setting this vinegar aside), and dropped them into the bowl with the rest of the ingredients. She then poured in some of the leftover vinegar and let it all soak for about 3 hours. With that out of the way, she got on to washing the 25 mackerels thoroughly in more vinegar, getting rid of all impurities and throwing the used vinegar away.

Now came our part. She began to grind the masala vigorously, continually adding vinegar until the spicy, red paste reached a smooth consistency. Once ready, she used part of the masala to coat the fish and then carefully placed them in a large, brown and white ceramic jar called a buyão that she had picked up during her visit to the weekly market. Once they were in place, she poured in the rest of the diluted masala until the fish was completely submerged. She sniffed at the contents and smiled - a few months and her para would be ready for eating. She was twisting the lid of the jar to make sure it was air tight when she suddenly remembered something her grandmother always did. Draping a piece of old cloth over the lid, she secured it around the neck of the jar with some sutli. It would help the para breathe for a few days.

By the time Milagrin was done, it was almost tea time. Placing the jar filled with para on one of the upper shelves, she decided to make herself a well-deserved cup of tea and watch the world go by from her balcão.

                     Perviz De Souza

Chapter 18

Balchão - pickling prawns

Milagrin rushed into the house full of excitement. One of the boys from the neighbourhood had come with the news that there was a bumper catch on the beach nearby. Apparently, the ramponkars (traditional fishermen) had drawn in a net bursting to the brim with jumbo prawns and were selling them quite cheap. Milagrin picked up a small pantulo and ran. She returned home after a while, her basket full of shrimp. Her husband was in the kitchen as she walked in, and seemed pleased to see not just his wife, but the basket of prawns she carried.

"That's a lot of prawns, Milagrin. You could make some balchão and save it for the monsoons." He said with gleaming eyes, almost smacking his lips thinking of his favourite delicacy.

"That's exactly what I planned to do," replied Milagrin. "Let me get to work."

Squatting on the bankim that was permanently at our side, she began the laborious task of cleaning and deveining the prawns while continuing her chatter with her husband. Then to our surprise, she began to toss the heads and shells at us. Her husband looked on in confusion. "Why are you doing that?" He asked, perplexed.

"I'll grind them and get some juice," she replied. "It will make a good stock for the curry."

As soon as she was done with the cleaning, she ground the shells and drew the juice through a piece of muslin cloth. I hated it; the smell was horrible. I was glad when she washed us clean. But our part was not over yet.

She began to toss the ingredients for her masala into the malti.

- 24 Kashmiri chilies
- 1 inch ginger
- 6 garlic cloves
- 1 and 1/2 teaspoons cumin
- 1/2 teaspoon turmeric powder
- 1 teaspoon black peppercorns
- 1/2 teaspoon cloves
- 1/2 inch cinnamon stick
- A small ball of tamarind
- 200 ml palm vinegar

Now she began to grind. Dakto and me were accustomed to the fiery chilies and the rich spices that went into most of Milagrin's masalas along with the strong, acidic flavour of the vinegar. All that heat and acid had little effect on us, but I am sure that her hands could feel the heat as she worked on these pastes. As was the case with many of her preparations, Milagrin did not use any water while grinding, but added vinegar in small portions until she had the paste ground to a smooth consistency. And then, as always, she washed off the curry using the remaining vinegar. But the strong smell hung around us and in her kitchen for the rest of the day.

Then came the actual cooking of the balchão. Milagrin first got the remaining ingredients ready.

- 4 medium onions, chopped fine
- 1/2 inch ginger, chopped fine
- 6 cloves of garlic, cut fine
- 2 green chilies, split open
- 2 sprigs of fresh karipata (curry leaves)
- About 500 ml of cooking oil
- Sugar and salt for seasoning

Setting her tizal on the fire, she first sauteed the prawns that she had washed and salted earlier, until they were well done. Setting

      Perviz De Souza

those aside for later, she poured some more oil into the tizal and tossed in the curry leaves. The pungent odour of the curry leaves permeated the air. She added in the chopped ginger and garlic, and continued frying until they began turning brown. After this, she added in the onions and continued to cook gently until the onions were really soft and started to caramelize. Now was the time to add in the masala and fry that as well. Milagrin kept her eyes on the pan, knowing she had to watch the cooking of the rich mixture until it was just right - when the oil began to separate - and then add in the fried prawns. She dropped in the two split green chilies for a little more heat and continued frying, all the while ensuring that she had enough oil in the mixture. She tasted it and sprinkled a little sugar for sweetness. The trick her mother had taught her was to have the oil floating on the top for the balchão. That way it would preserve itself and stay well throughout the monsoons.

She took the tizal off the fire and let her balchão cool. Milagrin began scrounging around in her little storeroom. She knew she had an empty buyão somewhere to store the pickled prawns.

Chapter 19

Crab Xec Xec

A part of the bargain when Milagrin picked up the prawns for the balchão, were a dozen or so large and heavy sea crabs. As soon as the balchão was ready and left to cool, she sat on the umor (steps) leading to the backyard and began cleaning the crabs. She pulled out the carapace (hard top shell) until she could see the inside of the crab. Taking out both its guts and gills, she deftly split the crab into two. Tearing apart the bigger claws, she cracked them open with a little polished stone she always had at hand as an emergency pounder. Once all the crabs were cleaned, she washed them, seasoned them with a little salt and set them aside.

Now, as with every Goan dish, she had to get the masala ready.

We watched as Milagrin pulled out her assortment of spice bottles and jars, wondering what would be different in this curry. This one was interesting as it involved roasting the ingredients before grinding them.

She carefully organised the ingredients across the kitchen table.

- 1 and 1/2 cup fresh grated coconut
- 1/2 teaspoon turmeric
- 1 medium onion (chopped)
- 6 garlic cloves (chopped)
- 1 inch piece of fresh ginger (chopped)
- 12 Kashmiri chilies
- 2 tablespoons coriander seeds
- 1 teaspoon cumin seeds
- 1/2 teaspoon peppercorns
- 6 cloves
- Salt and sugar for seasoning

This done, she soaked a small ball of tamarind in half a cup of hot water to extract the pulp and began her masala preparation.

On a hot kail, she roasted the coconut until it began to brown. Adding the turmeric powder, she roasted it some more. Once ready, she poured the mixture into a malti and proceeded to roast the onions next together with the garlic and ginger until they browned, and set them aside. Next to be roasted were the Kashmiri chilies, and finally the spices - coriander, cumin, pepper and cloves.

Returning to her bankim, she poured the roasted ingredients into my varn and began to grind, adding tamarind water until she had a coarse paste. I realised that though the masala had the smell and texture of the xacuti she had made before, it had its own unique character. Milagrin scooped out the paste and then washed away the remaining with water, setting this water aside.

She was in a rush as she had to get the crabs ready for lunch. She quickly diced a small onion and began to saute that in a touli with a few spoons of her home-made coconut oil. Adding two chopped chilies when the onion turned brown, she dropped in the crabs and let them cook for a few minutes before pouring in the masala. Milagrin let this simmer for a while as she seasoned it with a little salt and sugar.

Calling out to her husband, she said, "It's xit, sungttanchi koddi and xec xec for lunch. Come and eat while it's hot!"

Her husband walked in, lifted the lid off the touli and inhaled the rich aroma. "Dev borem korum, Milagrin. My mouth is watering, I can't wait to eat!"

Chapter 20

Patoleo in the making

It was the month of June, a time to celebrate the traditional feasts of St. Anthony, St. John the Baptist and of Sts. Peter and Paul. Traditionally, the new bride came back to her parent's home before the first rains and returned only after the feast of São João, which is why it is often called Zanvoichem Fest in Goa.

However, this year, the feast of São João was also a celebration of new life. Milagrin's son, Inas, was born earlier that year and as was the custom with a new baby in the house, she would have to make something special for the São João celebrations, which was the next day. The tradition demanded that every family make some patoleos - a Goan delicacy also prepared for the Feast of Our Lady of Assumption and the Konsachem Fest.

Patoleos are quite simple and relatively easy to make. This aromatic and steamed sweet is made in a base of rice paste spread over a fresh, turmeric leaf. It is usually filled with a stuffing of freshly grated coconut and Goan palm jaggery.

Having made them a dozen times before, Milagrin had her ingredients ready in a few minutes.

- 200 grams of Goan red rice or par boiled rice
- 1 fresh coconut (grated)
- 2 pyramids Goan palm jaggery (grated)
- Cardamoms (peeled & powdered)

She had soaked the rice a few hours earlier and now sitting on her bankim, she began to grind the rice into a fine paste. We noticed that she hardly added any water as she wanted the consistency of the paste to be firm and dense. Once done, she rolled the dough into a ball and placed it in a malti. After this, she proceeded to wash us thoroughly; Milagrin detested a messy grinding stone!

Perviz De Souza

She then mixed the grated coconut and jaggery in a touli. Setting it on the fire, she let this mixture cook for a while until it thickened. Tasting the mixture, she seasoned it with a little salt and then mixed in the ground cardamom.

Now to get working on stuffing the leaves.

In the corner of the backyard, like most Goan houses, Milagrin had a little plot for seasonal vegetables and turmeric plants. She skipped across and picked up a dozen fairly large turmeric leaves. After washing them thoroughly, she trimmed away the stalk and tip of the leaf, wiping them dry.

Milagrin kneaded the dough again and broke it up into small balls. Then, on the plain side of the turmeric leaf, she gently spread the dough with her fingers creating an even layer - making sure to avoid the edges of the leaf. Spreading a good helping of the coconut-jaggery filling, she folded the leaf along its length and pressed the edges down until it was well sealed. In a few minutes, she had all the leaves stuffed and ready for steaming.

Milagrin set the copper komfro or steamer on the fire and gently placed the patoleos inside. As the steam began cooking through the dough, the sweet fragrance of the turmeric leaves filled the kitchen. In about 25 minutes, the delicious sweetmeat was ready. She got her dhali ready, placing a crochet cloth into a shallow basket and artistically arranged the patoleos inside along with some mango, jackfruit and pineapple Now she had to await the São João revelers - they would be here soon.

Chapter 21

Sorak on a rainy day

In our years on the slopes of the ghats, we had experienced some torrential downpours, so when the rains came down in Goa, we were not really worried. In any case, we were safely ensconced in the warmth of Milagrin's kitchen. However, our joy was short-lived. The furiously flowing water hit the roof, pushing its way through the tiles and was soon dripping right over me.

Fortunately, Milagrin was in the kitchen and reacted quickly. Taking a kelken (a long bamboo pole used for plucking fruit), she carefully jogged the displaced tile back into place and within minutes the dripping came to a stop. Her husband walked in, soaked to the skin and dripping water all over the kitchen floor. Apparently, he had gone off to get some groceries, but due to the heavy rains, there was no fish in the market. In fact, there were hardly any vendors at the village tinto (marketplace).

"We have some kharem (dried fish)," said Milagrin. "I will make a sorak and roast some dry mackerel over the fire." Her husband really had no choice in the matter - at this stage of the monsoons, beggars couldn't be choosers.

As we watched, Milagrin grated a whole coconut into a malti and threw in the spices.

- 8 Kashmiri chilies
- 1 tablespoon coriander seeds
- 1 teaspoon cumin seeds
- 1 tsp black peppercorns
- 4 large cloves of garlic
- 1/2 teaspoon turmeric powder

And then, she got to the grinding.

                    Perviz De Souza

The smell of the masala told us that it was not too different from her usual coconut curry, but we were sure that our pretty lady would have some trick up her sleeve.

Once done with the grinding, she chopped 2 medium sized onions and dropped them into the hot oil in the kunnllem that was placed on the fire earlier. Sauteing the onions until they were soft and translucent, Milagrin added in two slit chilies and the ground curry paste. Pouring in two cups of plain water, she frequently checked its consistency. When it came to a boil, she added a cup full of tamarind water.

Once the curry began to bubble, Milagrin went to the sideboard and picked up the zaad piko ambo (tree-ripened mango) that had fallen off the tree during last night's storm. She peeled and cut the firm flesh into thin slices, adding it into the pot along with the seed.

"That was different." I thought to myself. The semi-ripe mango would add a delicious sour-sweet hit to the tangy, red curry.

Chapter 22

Khatkhatem – a vegetable curry

By early August, the seasonal vegetables were ready for picking. Though Milagrin wasn't much of a gardener, her husband was blessed with a green thumb. At the onset of the monsoons, he had sown seeds in their little kitchen garden. Now his work had borne fruit and we watched Milagrin come in from her garden with a pantulo full of fresh vegetables. Her husband looked at her and said, "Moga (sweetheart), why don't you make some khatkhatem? I'm going to the market and will bring back some more vegetables."

"I can," Milagrin replied, "but make sure you get some katta-konong (yam), because the khatkhatem is just not right without it."

Milagrin picked up her umbrella and walked out with her husband. "I will ask Swati for her recipe."

The two returned home within minutes of each other, her husband laden with a poti (cloth bag) stuffed with greens and Milagrin brandishing a scrap of paper on which she had scribbled out the recipe from Swati.

It was nice to see the husband and wife team up to work in the kitchen. While Milagrin called out the ingredients, her husband neatly laid them out on the old kitchen table.

The ingredients from Swati's recipe.

- 1/4 cup chopped yam
- 1/4 cup chopped sweet potatoes
- 1/4 cup chopped potatoes
- 1/4 cup chopped yellow pumpkin
- 1/4 cup chopped green plantain

- 1/4 cup chopped white radish
- 1/4 cup chopped green papaya
- 1 drumstick, chopped
- 1/4 cup white dry peas, soaked
- 10 dried temflan (Goan Sichuan pepper berries)
- 1 cup grated coconut
- 12 black peppercorns
- 4 green chilies
- 1/4 teaspoon turmeric powder
- 1 teaspoon chili powder
- 2 tablespoons grated jaggery
- 3 tablespoons tamarind pulp
- 1 teaspoon rice flour
- Salt for seasoning

Swati too was particular about her recipe and had asked that Milagrin follow it exactly.

She cracked the temflan berries and set them aside. Sitting across the adollo, she grated a full coconut and poured it into my varn. Adding in the peppercorns and green chilies, she ground them into a smooth paste with practiced movements, using water as necessary. Once done, she washed us thoroughly and moved onto the next task.

Milagrin first boiled the vegetables and peas in a fairly large kunnllem and then added in the turmeric and chili powder along with the jaggery, tamarind pulp, rice flour and salt, giving it a good stir. Next, she added in the ground coconut paste, the temflan berries and water until she had the right consistency and let that boil for a while.

In a few minutes, her khatkhatem was ready. Getting off the stool he was sitting on, her husband picked up a poie (a local fluffy brown bread). "Let me try some and give you my comments." He said with a cheeky smile. "Don't forget, you helped cook it too!" She replied, witty as always.

Chapter 23

The unique Samarachi Koddi

It had been raining cats and dogs all week, and the house was dark, damp and cold. Milagrin walked into the kitchen all bundled up and rummaged through the kitchen cabinet for her recipe book. She had a determined look in her eyes and we knew she had something planned.

Her husband walked in looking gloomy and grumpy and reached for the steaming bowl of pez (rice congee). "Can't we do something to brighten up the day?"

"I am planning to do something different. A good samarachi koddi should certainly cheer you up," Milagrin replied cheekily.

This curry is another of Goa's seasonal specials, made usually during the monsoons when fresh fish is not easily available. It is the combination of dried shrimp and fresh shrimp too, ambiachi solam (dried mango) and the roasted curry condiments that lend it a unique flavour.

Without wasting much time, she began putting her ingredients together.

- 2 cups dried shrimp
- A few fresh shrimp that had been bought at the manos (sluice gates) earlier that morning
- 1 onion (chopped)
- 3 pieces of dried mango and a paddo (seed)
- Salt for seasoning
- Coconut oil

And then into her maltulo went the masala ingredients:

- ¼ teaspoon grated nutmeg

- 2 pieces mace
- 1 inch piece of cinnamon
- 1 inch piece of ginger
- 4 garlic cloves
- 1 onion (chopped)
- 1 teaspoon cumin seeds
- 1/2 teaspoon fenugreek seeds
- 1/2 teaspoon turmeric powder
- 10 dry chilies
- 10 peppercorns
- 2 cups grated coconut
- 2 tablespoons coriander seeds
- 6 cloves
- Small piece of star anise

She also put a small ball of tamarind and the dried mango to soak in hot water.

Once her ingredients were ready, she roasted each of the spices on a hot kail and then did the same with onions, ginger and garlic, 1 cup coconut and the dried shrimp. She poured the still warm ingredients (except the dry shrimp) into my varn and quickly ground that into a thick paste.

Milagrin ground the second cup of grated coconut and extracted a thick milk, setting that aside in a maltulo.

She placed a kunnllem on the fire and sauteed the chopped onion until it turned a light brown. Next went in the curry paste and when that began to splutter, Milagrin added in two cups of water to get a good consistency and left that to boil. She then dropped in the dried mango and added the thick coconut milk and let the curry boil until the mango began to soften.

She poured in the tamarind extract and checked that the acidity was the way she liked it.

As the rich aroma of the boiling curry filled the kitchen, Milagrin dropped in the few fresh shrimp and a few minutes later added the dry shrimp. She let the curry continue boiling for about 10 minutes, allowing it to thicken. Testing a little of the curry on the palm of her hand, she smiled.

She was done.

 Perviz De Souza

Chapter 24

The traditional Fish Hooman

Sitting in our corner, we came to learn the many secrets of Goan cuisine. From the many conversations in Milagrin's kitchen, I learnt that though there were general recipes for most of the Goan delicacies, these were not written in stone. In fact, the style of cooking differed from family to family. These 'grandmother's recipes' were zealously guarded and passed down from generation to generation.

Milagrin loved to cook and was always looking to bring something new to her table. As much as she loved to cook the traditional Christian dishes, she also enjoyed trying out those that were popular amongst the Hindu community. At the dinner table yesterday, we heard her discussing the hooman she had tasted at a neighbour's house. She was planning to try out the recipe she had learnt.

This morning, her husband had brought home a small kingfish. Milagrin sat at her adollo and quickly cleaned the fish, cutting it into slices. She washed and seasoned the fish, setting it aside.

Returning to the adollo, she grated a coconut - essential for the curry paste.

Taking the malti with the coconut, she began to add in the remaining ingredients, regularly referring to her recipe book.

- 2 cups of onions, chopped
- 1 inch piece of ginger
- 7 red chilies
- 1 tablespoon cumin seeds
- A few bhirindam solam (kokum)

Returning to her bankim, she ground this into a thin, dry paste.

After finishing the grinding, Milagrin returned to the fish and marinated it in 2 teaspoons of turmeric powder and a garlic paste she had prepared earlier, letting that sit for about 15 minutes.

She then deep fried the pieces of fish in coconut oil and kept them aside.

And now for the cooking phase.

Milagrin added a chopped onion to the touli and sauteed it in two tablespoons of coconut oil until it was nice and brown. She added the ground masala paste and a teaspoon of turmeric powder, stirring it for a while and then poured in three cups of water, along with a few pieces of bhirindam solam or kokum. Once the gravy came to a boil, the pre-fried fish pieces were carefully dropped and allowed to cook for another 5 minutes.

Her hooman was ready!

       Perviz De Souza

Chapter 25

Ros Kaddunk - the bath with coconut milk

Over 25 years have passed since we arrived at Milagrin's house. In this time, a lot has changed in the kitchen. As the family has grown, so have their needs. Milagrin's is a fairly affluent family and at some point last year, a mechanised grinder made its appearance in the kitchen. Dakto and I have been left to ourselves for months now. It sure is demeaning to know that you are no longer wanted. A thin layer of soot and dust has settled over us and my varn is collecting bits and pieces of dirt. Although the kitchen remained busy, our corner was seldom visited any more.

In the midst of the gloom, there suddenly appeared a thin ray of light. Milagrin's son, Inas, would soon be married and we could hear the details of the lavish celebration that was being planned for their eldest son. Milagrin sat with her family, finalising the menu for the big day. However, first was the traditional pre-wedding Ros.

We learnt that in Goan weddings, it was customary for the families of the bride and groom to separately hold a ceremonial bath for them at their respective houses. This custom usually took place a day or two before the traditional wedding.

The ros kaddunk ceremony involves the application of a cupful of pure, coconut juice on the head, face and hands of the groom or bride. Milagrin was determined that in keeping with the tradition, the coconut would be ground on the rogddo. We were exhilarated to hear this news! One of the neighbours explained that the groom-to-be would need to come into the nahnni or little bathroom in the kitchen, to have his bath after the ros. We would at least get to see Inas covered in coconut milk. We couldn't believe that the little boy we had seen growing up was soon to be married. How time flies!

Milagrin herself sat and grated the coconut. We were happy to go through the rotatory motions; a movement and pace we had become accustomed to over the years. Once she was satisfied with the consistency of the paste, Milagrin strained the thick juice through a muslin cloth. That evening, dressed in one of her finest outfits, she picked up the bowl of milk and went out into the sitting room for the ceremony. She would not be the first to apply the ros for her son. Her mother-in-law was visiting and as the oldest member of the family, she would have that privilege. After her, it would be Milagrin's turn and others would follow.

We could not see what was happening, but we could hear the melodious voices of the women (interrupted by a couple of false notes from the men), singing the zoti or verses in honour of the groom-to-be.

Amrutani ross-su,
Bab to paim-ia tall asum'
Tuje Pai/Mai tuka ross laitam,
Bore bhaxen to gans-su.*

Then the entire group walked into the kitchen, where the large tambeachem bhannd (copper pot used for heating water) was on the boil. As Inas stepped into the nahnni for his bath, the songs continued. We could hear the tinkle of coins being dropped into the pot and were really happy to be a part of Inas' wedding preparations.

*Source unknown

    Perviz De Souza

Epilogue

It's been a good 50 years since we made that long journey from the mountain side in the ghat section. For many years after being moved to Milagrin's home, Ghanpath would pass by the village calling "taaki, taaki", reminding the villagers that their stones needed to be chipped again to ease the grinding process. He and one of his sons (or grandsons), would then carry us out into the compound in an all-purpose jute sack, to the shade of the giant mango tree. There, they would spend an hour or two, gently and skillfully chipping us with a small chisel until our surfaces were a little rougher again. Once they were done, Milagrin would put us through the curing process once more.

However, it's been many years since we have heard from Ghanpath. We really miss seeing his rugged and weather-beaten face. With the passage of time and the arrival of technology, the demand for his grinding stones has dropped considerably. I am sure he must be well into his years now.

Milagrin's kitchen too has felt the influence of technology. Since she acquired an electric grinder, she finds the need for her rogddo only occasionally - usually to grind her recheado masala. She may have aged but her culinary skills are still the stuff of legend. Like Milagrin, we too have aged and matured. Having watched her at work for a lifetime, we too have amassed a wealth of culinary knowledge.

On her good days, she sits at the stone and grinds some of her favourite pastes, her hands moving with practiced ease, although we can see from her expressions that her bodily strength is not the same anymore. On other days, one of her daughters will run the grinder and a loud humming sound fills the room. On the electric grinder, the task doesn't take that long and it's definitely less work.

Over the years, the kitchen too has changed - the old fireplace replaced with a gas stove. Aluminum and steel pots and pans have replaced clay and copper ones on the shelves. But Milagrin will always reminisce about the old days and say with a sigh, "There's nothing like a curry ground on my rogddo and cooked on a wood fire in my favourite tizal!"

                    Perviz De Souza

Glossary of Konkani Kitchen Terminology*

Adollo - A curved metal blade fixed to a low wooden stool used for cleaning fish, dicing vegetables, meat, etc. The tip of the adollo is rounded into a serrated grater and is called Kantollem. It is used for grating coconut and the process is called chun kantunk.

Amaldosto - A brass pounder or mortar and pestle.

Bankim - A small low wooden stool usually placed next to the rogddo.

Bannxirem - A rag that worked as a pot holder and even a duster.

Bhannd - A fairly large earthen pot used for storing par-boiled rice or paddy.

Budkulo - A small clay pot normally used for brewing tea and medical potions.

Buwiao - A large, brown and white ceramic jar with a screw-on lid.

Chimmto - A pincer for removing anything placed for roasting on the fire or for moving coal.

Chul - Traditional fireplace made with three stones

Dantem - A set of millstones generally used for grinding cereals and pulses.

Dhai - A wooden ladle for making sweets.

Dhonnanchem Kodhem - A large earthen container usually kept just outside the kitchen into which all the kitchen food waste was disposed.

Donndul - A medium sized earthen pot used for storing rice and other cereals.

Fatnicho Fator - A cylindrical granite stone that is about a foot in length and 3-4 inches in diameter. It is used as a roller with both hands to grind masalas on the fatorn.

Fatorn - A flat five-sided granite stone with raised edges used for grinding masala.

Funkpachi Nolli - A small metal or bamboo pipe used to coax the fire in the chul (fireplace).

Chimnecho Divo - A glass kerosene lamp.

Garrafão - A glass bottle of 5 litres used to store feni or vinegar.

Ghonnsunneacho or Rogddeacho Fator - An oblong granite stone carved to fit the varn on the ghonnsunno/rogddo. In order to grind the masala, the ingredients are filled in the varn and the fator is placed in it. The tip of the fator is held with either hand and rotated in a clockwise or anti-clockwise motion, until the masala is ground to the desired consistency.

Ghonnsunno or Rogddo - A large bowl-shaped granite stone with a varn (hole) carved out in the middle. It is used for grinding.

Gurguret - A terracotta drinking water pot usually shaped as a rooster with the head as a spout.

Kail - A deep frying pan usually made of copper.

Kailontto - A metal ladle.

Kantto - A fork used for testing roast meat.

Koddiecho Doulo or Doulo - A ladle made of a polished coconut shell with a bamboo handle, normally used for serving curries or gravy.

Koddo - A small outdoor barn located just outside the kitchen, used for storing paddy.

Koito - A small multi-purpose machete used for everything from cutting wood, splitting coconuts to chopping fish and meat.

Kollso - A big pot usually made of copper, but sometimes of clay.

     Perviz De Souza

Kollsuli - A small earthen or copper pot.

Komfro - A fairly large dome-shaped copper steamer used for preparing sannas, patoleo, pudde, sirvoieo and other steamed specialties.

Konnffo - A wooden contraption on which the xitacho budkulo (rice pot) was tilted for draining rice water.

Kotti - A polished coconut shell used to scoop out water, especially when grinding on a rogddo.

Kuler - A tablespoon.

Kulerin - A teaspoon.

Kunnllem - A medium-sized, flat clay vessel used for preparing curry.

Kurponn - A round bamboo or wooden lid used to cover a budkulo or other clay pots.

Lattnni - A wooden rolling pin used for rolling chapattis or dough.

Malti - A large clay bowl.

Maltulo - A small clay bowl.

Mandd - A round, flat wooden lid with a small handle.

Mannon - A small clay pot used for serving pezz (congee or rice gruel).

Matis - A match box.

Moddki - A medium-sized clay pot used for cooking rice.

Moddko - A larger clay pot used for boiling water.

Mussoll - A round, wooden pole approximately 6-7 feet in height and 3-4 inches in diameter used for husking rice.

Niunnem - A thick ring made of tightly-bound hay on which were placed clay vessels.

Pantulo - A small bamboo basket.

Pittachi Mannd - A board for rolling chapattis. Some housewives would use a table top or any flat surface.

Ponti or Ghasletticho Divo - A lamp made out of a small bottle.

Shinkear - A suspended larder made of rope usually with a 'niunnem' at the bottom.

Sup - A large bamboo pan, used either for cleaning grain or to get rid of chaff from husked paddy.

Suri - A kitchen knife of medium size.

Tambeachem Bhannd - A very large copper pot used for heating water for the entire family.

Tambio - A small copper pot used during a bath or washing.

Tizal - A large, flat clay vessel for cooking large quantities, especially meats.

Touli - A shallow clay utensil.

Tovo - A flat earthen pan used for frying chapatti, bakreo or kailoieo. These vanished with the coming of metal fry pans.

Varn - A round hole in the floor of a kitchen, about 6-7 inches in diameter and 7 inches deep into which rice is husked.

Vattli - A brass plate.

Xitachi moddki - A pot used for cooking rice.

Xitacho Doulo - A ladle made of a polished coconut shell with a bamboo stick used for serving rice.

*

*Fernandes, Domnic. "[Goanet] A GENERAL KITCHEN OF THE 50's AND THE 60's!" The Mail Archive, 3 Oct. 2004, www.mail-archive.com/goanet@goanet.org/msg16975.html.